THE AFRO HAIR & BEAUTY BIBLE

This book is dedicated to women of colour everywhere

First published in Great Britain in 2010 by
Creative Forma Publishing

ISBN 978-0-9564791-0-5

Pictures: iStock Photo
Designed by: Alison Husbands

Alison Husbands is herby identified as the author of this work in accordance with
Section 77 of the Copyright, Designs & Patents Act 1988.

Readers are advised to carry out their own research before trying any new products or methods. The Afro hair & Beauty Bible does not accept any responsibility and or liability for any adverse affects the reader may have experienced.

CONTENTS PAGE

INTRODUCTION

MY HAIR JOURNEY

I first started my quest for beautiful long and healthy hair in 2004. After years dry, brittle and damaged Relaxed hair I turned to wearing weaves in order to obtain a more polished and presentable look.

I remember getting ready for my day in the mornings, I would style my hair and I would find short broken hairs all over my clothes. I soon learned that in order to prevent having to change my outfit twice I would have to drape a shawl around my shoulders to catch all the broken hairs.

I was first introduced to weaves when a friend of mine was getting married, another friend and myself were both bridesmaids so we paid a visit to the hair salon to get our hair styled together. She was a frequent half weave wearer and advised me what hair to buy and how many rows would be suitable and the most natural looking. And that was the beginning; I continued wearing weaves (usually 4-5 rows) for about 6 years, over the years as I learned the process I upgraded the quality of hair and eventually learned how to do the whole process myself.

It wasn't until I was going to go on holiday to Barbados that I decided enough was enough with the weave wearing and I took it out and wore my hair free. It felt weird at first not to have the taught canerows on the back and sides of my head, however my hair was full, thick and healthy or so I thought, at this point my hair sat just past my shoulders with a side fringe.

Over the duration of my holiday my hair was saturated with sea water, sand and heat, it went through vigorous combing and air drying which left my hair frizzy. When I returned home the ends of my hair were dry and straw like; I brought several hot oil treatments that I assumed would fix the problem which it did not so I gave my hair a good trim, my hair then felt in better condition and easier to manage. I thought my problem was resolved; I wore my short flicked-out hairstyle for a few months before the problem came back. I then had to cut a further two inches off (4 inches in total in 3 months) before I went on to the internet and started to research alternative solutions to my hair dilemma.

I found various online communities full of women of colour like myself who displayed pictures of themselves with hair down their back! I thought "this can't be possible; they must be weaves" but after a while of reading about their hair care practices I realised what they had to say made sense. I became fixated with hair; I was constantly reading up on hair; whether it was online, books or magazines; whatever there was to know about hair care I wanted to know it.

This new interest of mine also left quite a dent in my pocket; I remember being so excited when Saturday's came round to visit the afro hair shop and buying the latest product that I read was a must have product. I learnt through trial and error what products to use and what ones to avoid.

As a result of my hair fixation I have become quite an expert on the topic and I would like to share my knowledge and experiences with other women of colour who are now where I once was.

I hope you find this book helpful, insightful and you enjoy reading it as much as I have enjoyed writing it.

Alison x

HAIR CARE

THE AFRO HAIR STRUCTURE

Many people believe that Afro hair is dramatically different to all other hair types, on the surface it is but the basic make up of our hair is the same as any other hair type. The hair structure itself is made up of several components as follows:

The Cuticle

This is the outer layer of the hair. It is made up of layer upon layer of transparent cells that interlock forming one complete unit (think of a roof made up of thousands of tiles). The thickness of the cuticle can vary, in Afro hair the cuticle tends to be up to twice the thickness of European hair, however Afro hair has less layers of cuticles therefore is vulnerable to moisture loss and breakage.

The Cortex

This is the middle layer of the hair shaft. It is made up of cells which are compressed together and intertwined with one another. The Cortex is what provides the hair with the strength and elasticity it needs. The Cortex is easily manipulated with the use of various chemicals and heat.

Melanin

Is what gives your hair and skin its colour, the more Melanin you have the darker your hair is. The Melanin is sandwiched within the Cortex of the hair.

The Follicle

This is the part of the hair that sits below the scalp, the healthier the Follicle is the healthier the hair will be once it emerges from the scalp.

Sebaceous & Sudoniferous Glands

These glands sit below the scalp. The Sebaceous glands release oil into the follicle and onto the scalp and the Sudoriferous glands release small amounts of sweat which contains salts, acids, water and bacteria. This combination can cause dandruff and itchy scalps if left to their own devices.

As you know hair can vary from straight to curly. A universal way of categorising hair is by using the Hair Typing Classification System as follows:

First Classifier
This is the most obvious breakdown of the three categories.

Straight Hair
1a   Bone straight
1b   Straight but with a slight volume to it.
1c   Straight but with a slight volume and a few waves usually at the nape of neck or temples

Wavy Hair
2a   Loose S-wavy hair
2b   Shorter, more defined S-waves
2c   More distinct S-waves with some spiral curls forming

Curly Hair
3a   Big, loose spiral curls
3b   Medium bouncy ringlets
3c   Tight corkscrews

Afro Hair
4a   Very tightly coiled small S-curls
4b   Extremely tightly coiled small S-curls

Second Classifier
This category determines what the majority of your individual strands of hair looks like.

Fine
Thin strands that sometimes are almost translucent when held up to the light. Shed strands can be hard to see even against a contrasting background. Fine hair is difficult to feel or it feels like an ultra-fine strand of silk.

Medium

Strands are neither fine nor coarse. Medium hair feels like a cotton thread. You can feel it, but it is not stiff or rough. It is neither fine nor coarse.

Coarse

Strands usually are easily identified against most backgrounds. Coarse hair feels hard and wiry. As you roll it back and forth, you may actually hear it.

Third Classifier

This category determines your overall amount of strands of hair.

To determine the amount of hair you have on your head and which category your hair falls into; put your hair in a ponytail with as much hair as possible in it. Now measure the circumference of the ponytail with a tape measure.

I	Thin (less than 2 inches / 5 centimeters)
II	Normal (between 2-4 inches / 5-10 centimeters)
III	Thick (more than 4 inches /10 centimeters)

Afro hair tends to be rather dry, especially in comparison to straighter hair. With 1a type hair the oils from the follicle have no problems sliding along the hair shaft moisturising the hair as it goes; however with Afro hair the oils gets trapped at every bend and curve so the natural oils cannot coat and penetrate into the main bulk of the hair shaft, this is one of the many reasons why the ends of the hair seem so much dryer than the root of the hair. Afro hair typically absorbs 10 – 15% less moisture than any other type of hair therefore it is extremely important to keep the hair well moisturised.

Afro hair is a very unique hair type and requires methods and products that most other hair types would not use. Afro hair is very fragile and easy to break that is why it needs so much extra care and attention.

AFRO HAIR MYTHS

There are many Do's and Don'ts in circulation in the black community about hair. Good and bad practices are passed along from mother, daughter, aunties, cousins, sisters, friends and professionals. Much of this advice does far more harm than good. Some common misconceptions are listed below:

You can't wash your hair too much or it will fall out
Washing your hair will not cause it to fall out; frequent washing can improve the condition of your hair

Water will dry out your hair
Water will not dry out your hair; some harsh shampoo's can strip your hair of its natural moisture.

Black women can't grow long hair
Any person can grow long hair regardless of their race. Only illnesses such as Alopecia can prevent a person from growing hair.

Relaxed hair can't grow long
Relaxed hair can grow just as any other hair type; however Relaxed hair has more trouble holding onto moisture.

Dry hair is damaged by too frequent washing
Dry hair is further damaged by not enough moisture (water) in the hair.

I can't let my hair get wet
Water is VERY important to the hair; it is wise to frequently get your hair wet.

My hair is thick and course it can handle anything
Afro hair is the most fragile hair type, even course Afro hair is more delicate than wavy Mediterranean hair.

Grease will stop my itchy scalp
Grease clogs pores and the hair follicles, preventing your scalp from repairing and lubricating itself. Traditional grease containing Petroleum does far more harm than good.

Dirty hair grows faster than clean hair
Dirty hair does not grow any faster, in fact the build up of products, sweat, oil and dead skin cells prevent beneficial ingredients from entering the hair hindering new growth.

Only biracial women can grow long hair
All hair can grow to long lengths, 3c hair (which is the most common hair type amongst biracial women) is less prone to breakage than Afro 4b hair therefore it can retain the length of the hair better.

Petroleum and mineral oil must be good for Afro hair as it is in all of the black hair products
Petroleum and mineral oil is a very CHEAP man-made substitute for natural oils.

Cutting your hair makes your hair grow
Cutting the ends of your hair does not impact on the growth rate at the root of the hair. Cutting your hair gets rid of damaged ends that can creep up the hair damaging and breaking the bulk of the hair further.

Greasing my scalp will make my hair grow
Stimulating your scalp will encourage hair growth, the Grease does nothing apart give an artificial shine.

I can Relax over previously Relaxed hair as the ends are kinky.
Relaxing an area of hair more than once causes over processing, this in turn leads to dryness and breakage. 'Kinky' ends are a sign that your hair is dehydrated and needs moisture.

Products made for European hair will not work on my Afro hair type
Good quality hair products are designed for all hair types regardless of the race; choose products that are designed to combat a particular problem that you may have such as dandruff or dry damaged hair.   Often products aimed toward European consumers have better and healthier ingredients than those aimed at Afro consumers.

Afro hair is stronger than any other hair type
Afro hair is weaker than any other hair type and should be treated very delicately.

Braids and dreadlocks make my hair grow faster
Less / low manipulation can allow your hair grow to its full potential. Dreadlocks and braids allow the hair to work as a team rather than individual strands therefore making the hair appear stronger.

I can take my hair out of braids or weaves and put a Relaxer on it the next day

You can do this if you don't mind severe hair loss! You should always wait at LEAST one week before applying a Relaxer to hair that has recently been in braids.

Sleeping with wet hair causes scalp fungus

Sleeping with a scarf around wet hair is a good way to allow your hair to dry naturally. This will not cause fungus, your hair does not know if you are awake or asleep.

You can repair split ends

Split ends can be temporarily concealed with waxes and serums; however they cannot be repaired, you can prevent split ends from becoming worse by cutting them off.

My hair will break off if I don't retouch it every 6 weeks

It is a good idea to stretch out your Relaxer retouches as the 'run off' from the Relaxer in the neutralising stage can cause over processing and breakage to the rest of your hair. As long as the line of demarcation (the line where your Natural hair meets the Relaxed hair) is well moisturised and you are gentle whilst combing and styling your hair should not break. Missing every other Relaxer can do wonders for the health of your hair.

Hot oil treatments moisturise my dry hair

Most oils do not moisturise the hair, only water does.

My hair can only reach a certain length

Your hair can grow to whatever length you desire, just as long as you look after it.

I have bad hair

Hair is hair, your hair can be healthy or unhealthy but there is no such thing as Good or Bad hair only different hair types.

I have good hair so I will never have hair problems

Any hair type can have problems if it is not well looked after, even types 1 and 2.

Children's hair does not need much maintenance

Afro hair in general needs much more maintenance and care than European hair regardless of its age.

Natural hair is difficult and not very manageable
Natural hair can be very versatile, with the right products and techniques. Natural hair can be much easier to maintain than Relaxed hair.

Children's Relaxers are less harsh than regular Relaxers
Relaxers aimed at children are often exactly the same as Relaxers aimed at adults; they just have prettier packaging.

I don't have time to think about what I should use on my hair, I can just use anything
Setting aside 3 minutes a day to moisturise your hair can make a great deal of difference to the health of your hair. Spending 30 seconds to read the ingredients of what is in the product you are about to purchase can save you time and money in the long run.

I can leave Relaxer on for longer than the recommended time as I have thick hair and it needs to take
Relaxers are very strong and powerful chemicals, it is important to stick to the manufactures instructions. Leaving a Relaxer on for too long can cause burns or hair loss and bald patches!

As you can see all of the statements above are untrue, I will go into a more detailed breakdown of all of the above statements within the relevant chapters later on in this book.

AFRO HAIR TYPES

NATURAL HAIR

There are many misconceptions about Natural hair, often people believe that Natural hair is difficult to maintain and looks untidy. They assume that it is going to take a lot of time and effort to 'tame it' into looking good. In fact Natural hair is extremely versatile and fairly straight forward to manage as long and you are using the proper techniques and products. Often it is viewed that Natural 3c hair is easier to manage than Natural 4a hair, as with all hair types some patience is required yet each face their own challenges.

Every head of Natural hair is different and there is often different hair types on one head, it is important to spend time getting to know what your hair likes and does not like. The products a type 3c would use would be different to what a 4b head would use. Your friend may have Natural hair and a particular product may work wonders for her but not for you so it is important to find a few staple products that work with your own Natural hair.

As a woman with Natural hair; water and conditioners are going to be your closest friends, many women experience shrinkage when their hair gets wet however this is just your hair drinking up as much water as it can. The hair can shrink anywhere from 25 - 75%, when washing your hair; wash it in sections in 4 loose braids, this will allow you to wash without manipulating your hair to much which will help you to avoid tangles and knots. By allowing the hair to dry in the braids will lessen the amount of shrinkage making your hair appear longer. Applying a mixture of honey, molasses, bananas and apple cider vinegar as a treatment after shampooing can elongate the curl pattern and lessen the amount of shrinkage by up to 40%.

Detangling once a week is a good way to remove any knots without losing too much hair; it is fine to lose some hair as we all lose about 150 hairs per day. Naturals should avoid using bristle brushes on their hair and should never comb their hair when it is dry. Combing dry hair will cause you to lose your curl definition and your hair will look a frizzy mess. Instead comb your hair wet using conditioner or moisturiser with a wide toothed comb in sections working from the bottom of each section up to the root thoroughly detangling as you go.

Excessive tangling is a clear sign that you are in need of a trim. Take care with the ends of your hair and be sure to moisturise them well, seal in moisture each night with a little bit of your favorite oil and wrap your hair in a silk or satin scarf or bonnet.

As with all Afro hair heat should be used rarely, Natural hair is very versatile and can be styled in attractive styles without the use of heat. However it is achievable to have healthy hair and use heat weekly. Straightening Natural hair with ceramic irons is the safest and healthiest way to achieve straight styles; old fashioned hot combs often burn and singe the hair, once you damage Natural hair with heat it cannot be repaired, the curl pattern will never be the same again.

Before you begin it is important to wash and deep condition the hair for best results, apply a leave-in conditioner for added moisture and protection followed by a good heat protector such as *Chi Heat Protectant, Aveda Brilliant Damage* or *Sabino Moisture Block* (which is also a great anti humectant). To save on the over use heat of allow your hair to dry naturally in large plaits or twists. Then take your ceramic straightening iron; *Maxiglide* and *FHI Platform* straightening irons are very good on Natural Hair. Section your hair in 2 inch sections and go over each section no more than 3 times from root to tip in one fluid movement, this will allow your hair to have body and movement, no oil should be used on the hair before heat styling but always use a heat protector. Finally finish off with an anti humectant to prevent your Natural hair reverting; *Aveda Brilliant Anti-Humectant* is a great product to keep your straight style lasting as long as possible.

Growing out Relaxed hair to Natural hair is a long process that requires patience and dedication, it can take anywhere between 6 months and 2 years. The most important thing to remember is to handle your hair with care during this transitional stage as the line of Demarcation is very weak and is prone to breakage. This is why many women opt to cut off their Relaxed ends and leave only the Natural hair at the roots, this is a much easier way to Transition although there are other alternatives such as wearing braids, weaves, locks or twists, do not leave these in for too long as this may cause your hair to matt, try experimenting with hair styles that work for you.

Which ever method you choose it is important to keep your well moisturised. This means deep conditioning weekly and moisturising daily. Choose creamy conditioners, moisturisers and use heavier oils on the Natural hair such as *Shea Butter, Infusium Leave-In Conditioner* is a great conditioner to help ease tangles and care for the hair, try to use products that are sulphate free as these are far less drying on the hair. Learn what your hair likes by using good products that are going to enhance you hair but do steer away from products that contain alcohol.

AFRO HAIR TYPES

RELAXED HAIR

Many black women experience difficulties when trying to manage their Relaxed hair. They find that when their hair is freshly Relaxed it is soft, manageable and easy to maintain. However after a few weeks their hair turns dry and lacks shine along with the body it once had. So why is this?

Relaxers work by breaking down the protein bonds deep within the hair. These bonds give the hair its strength and structure. The chemicals in Relaxers are extremely strong and have a high pH level of 10 - 14. They are strong enough to literally transform the original structure of the hair by penetrating the cortex layer. The original curl pattern is then loosened or 'Relaxed' into a straighter texture.

The process of Relaxing the hair can be very damaging to the hair if done incorrectly. The central layer of the hair shaft provides the hair with its shape, elasticity and strength and it is this layer that is altered during the Relaxing process. This can lead to the hair becoming weak and brittle which leads to breakage and excess shedding.

Before even thinking about applying a Relaxer to your hair you have to prepare your hair first. In every box of home use Relaxer; the instructions warn "do not use on damaged hair", it is important to read the instructions and follow the advice given, if handled incorrectly Relaxers can be very dangerous, even though you may think it is unnecessary; reading the instructions properly can save you from losing your hair.

Many women turn to self-Relaxing, this can be very beneficial if you have the patience and understand exactly what you are doing. If you are going to take the plunge and take the health of your Relaxed hair into your own hands then it is a good idea to practice your Relaxing technique. Use a thick conditioner such as *Elasta QP DPR-11* in place of a Relaxer and apply the cream to the new growth (roots) only, this is a good way of practicing your skills without damaging your hair and will also allow you to determine exactly how long the application stage will take you. It is important to keep the Relaxer on the new growth only and not overlap it onto the previously Relaxed hair, when Relaxers are continuously applied to hair that has already been Relaxed this causes the hair to become weak and over processed therefore damaging the hair further.

I have explained how the protein bonds are broken down during the process therefore it is important to build up the protein in your hair as much as possible one week before hand to ensure that your hair is strong enough to handle the Relaxer. Products such as *Aphogee 2-Step Treatment for Damaged* hair provide the optimum level of protein in your hair before Relaxing.

Once you have prepared your hair keep the manipulation to a minimum, avoid scratching and irritating your scalp or tying your hair back too tightly. Do not wet your scalp or hair for at least five days before you begin Relaxing this is to create a natural barrier to protect your scalp from the strong chemicals.

After you have had a few practice applications you need to decide on what type of Relaxer works for you. There are 2 types of Relaxers, Lye and No-Lye. Lye Relaxers contain a chemical called Sodium Hydroxide, these Relaxers tend to be kinder to your scalp however far more drying on the hair. No-Lye Relaxers (please do not be fooled into thinking 'No-Lye' means 'no lie' and you will get better results!) contain Guanidine Hydroxide; this type of Relaxer is less drying on the hair however it does not get the hair as straight as Lye Relaxers.

So which one is right for you? As each head is different it is difficult to put each person in a particular category therefore it may take testing the two types to see which type works for your hair and scalp. Once you have found a Relaxer that suits you; stick to it. It is not wise to chop and change your Relaxers with each application this can cause serious damage to the hair as each type and brand is different to the next.

For extra sensitive scalps some women opt for using childrens Relaxers with the belief that they are less harsh than adult Relaxers, this is not the case and they often contain exactly the same ingredients as adult Relaxers. However there is a way to make your regular Relaxer kinder to sensitive scalps. You can add a few tablespoons of an oil such as olive oil or jojoba oil to the Relaxer; this dilutes the mixture and also slows down the process which will give you more application time.

The most efficient way to section your hair is in quarters, start from the area that is the most resistant. Take your time and work through each section whilst keeping an eye on the clock, aim to apply the Relaxer to each section within 2-3 minutes; taking care only to apply it to the new growth area. Now you have to focus on doing the straightening part by 'smoothing' the Relaxer along the new growth, go back to the point you started at as this point has been processing for the longest time. Some people like to use their gloved fingers to smooth the Relaxer however I prefer to use the back of a fine toothed comb and smooth each section

an inch at a time. Leave the hairline and nape of the neck to the end of the application step as these areas are the most fragile and needs less processing time. Be sure to stick to the time limit that the instructions advise for your hair type.

If your scalp begins to burn or tingle then that is not a good sign, this means that the Relaxer is now working on your scalp and breaking the hair down below the surface. This is why it is very important to base your scalp with a product such as *Vaseline* that will protect your scalp; this can be done the day before Relaxing. Relaxers should not cause you pain; if it does then wash it out immediately. When a Relaxer burns your scalp your scalp may start to weep this is when a clear liquid oozes out similar to what happens when you get a blister, in turn this will cause your hair to stick to your scalp and the scalp to scab over. This does not sound every nice and does not need to be a part of your regular Relaxer process as long as you follow the instructions and guidelines for the correct way to Relax your hair. If you do experience Relaxer burns gently soothe the area with cool water and natural Aloe Vera gel, do not pick or irritate any sore areas as this may cause the sore to become infected.

You should never Relax your hair until it is bone straight. Aim to retain a slight wave to the hair as the straighter the hair is Relaxed the weaker your hair will be in the long run, you can always achieve bone straight styles with ceramic straightening irons.

Rinse out the Relaxer using luke warm water and ensure all visible traces are out of your hair. It is important to keep the hair as straight as possible during this stage to ensure the cuticles lay straight and smooth. Next apply a light protein conditioner such as *Aphogee 2 Minute Reconstructor*, this is to restore the protein that has just been lost and will also initiate the neutralising process and bring your hair down to the normal level of pH 4.5 to 5.5. This is applied before shampooing as at this stage the cuticle is the most open and receptive to treatments.

You can then continue as normal and follow up with several lathers of a neutralising shampoo. Relaxers can continue to break down the hair for up to an hour, so it is important to ensure you get all of the Relaxer out. Not neutralising the hair properly can result in hair loss therefore it is wise to leave the shampoo to sit of your hair for 5 minutes for each lather and gently but thoroughly massage the scalp.

Sometimes the shampoo alone is not enough, a clever tip for thorough neutralisation is to apply a solution of 1 part apple cider vinegar to 10 parts water (add more water if you find this solution to strong), this will radically bring down the pH level from the Relaxer to normal level thereby quickly neutralising your hair in one step, follow up with an additional lather to get the excess out and the smell of the vinegar. Two lathers of shampoo (that has been left to sit on the hair for 5 minutes) followed by two rinses of the apple cider vinegar solution then one more lather is enough to thoroughly neutralise the Relaxer. Once the neutralising stage is completed apply a thick moisturising conditioner for 1 hour or longer as your hair has had quite an ordeal and needs plenty of moisture.

After the Relaxer process is completed ensure you wash your hair 5-7 days later and follow with a moisturising and protein conditioner such as *Organic Root Stimulator Replenishing Conditioner.*

Afro hair that has been Relaxed lacks even more moisture than Afro hair that is Natural. This means that Relaxed Afro hair needs extra moisture than Natural Afro hair therefore you should steer clear of products that contain silicones; these are present in some shampoos and conditioners as well as serums. Silicones coat the hair preventing moisture and other good ingredients from entering the hair.

Many women put the fate of their Relaxed hair into the hands of professionals; this is all very well but what if the professional in question does not fully understand the Relaxing process themselves, on the other hand there are fantastic qualified hair care professionals but sifting out the ones that are going to encourage your hair to thrive and grow healthy hair rather than the ones that are just going to make your hair look salon styled for a few days and leave you with a lifetime of unhealthy damaged hair is quite a chore.

Relaxed hair is very fragile so it is important to treat it with care, handle your Relaxed hair as you would an expensive silk blouse. When Relaxed hair is wet it becomes even more fragile and prone to snapping; take care when combing and tying up wet hair. Avoid using hair brushes as they can snag and cause wet hair to break; using a brush to tidy up the hairline is fine as long as it is done gently, there is nothing worse than balding edges.

Some women like to give their Relaxed hair a break and opt for weaves or braids, this can be beneficial, however it is important to give your hair the much needed care it needs after taking out any form of braids. Wait at least one week before retouching the new growth, during this week you will need to apply a protein reconstructor and deep moisturising treatments, making sure you have left ample time for your scalp to settle.

As with all Afro hair it is important to wrap your hair at night or sleep on a silk or satin pillowcase to prevent your hair rubbing against the coarse material of cotton.

The amount of heat that you use should be limited to once a week or less, blow dryers and straightening irons are direct heat methods and should be used in moderation and at a medium to low temperature. When using a straightening iron it is important to use one with the correct temperature for your hair type. Generally Relaxed hair can handle heat at a temperature of 250 - 300°F where as Natural hair and hair of other textures can use a higher heat of 400 - 450°F.

Relaxed hair can be styled effectively using indirect heat; hooded hair dryers teamed with large rollers are a great healthy alternative to achieving straight styles with little to no damage. Allowing your hair to dry naturally under a head scarf or in a secure bun is another good way to dry your with no heat damage.

Hair that is referred to as Texturised has undergone a chemical process that is similar to Relaxing or by leaving a Relaxer on for 10 minutes or less and not smoothing the product along the hair. Texturised hair retains some of the Natural curl pattern however it is somewhat looser. Type 4a/b hair that has been Texturised will be transformed into a similar state of 3c hair types. Hair that has undergone this chemical process should be treated the same as Relaxed hair, protein treatments and moisture balance is just as important to Texturised hair as it is to Relaxed hair.

Texturised hair can be left to dry naturally revealing is new texture, again heat should be limited but it can be used in the same way that Relaxed hair can use it. Rinsing Texturised hair daily can provide the optimum level of moisture whilst refreshing the look of your curls.

Hair that has been Texturised should use lightweight products and natural oils to lock in moisturiser and to define the looser curls.

As with Relaxed hair you will begin to see new growth and you will require touch ups; although not as often as Relaxed hair, aim to touch up your new growth once every three months, to preserve the curl pattern from being affected by the run off from the Relaxer or Texturiser during the application.

10 STEPS TO HEALTHY HAIR

1. MOISTURE

As women of colour we have been ingrained with the fear of water and the so called damaging effects it has on our hair.

Water is the most basic form of moisture, without sufficient water content our hair would be as dry as a desert. We need to have a good amount of water within our hair shaft order to maintain healthy well moisturised hair. Just as plants cannot grow without water; neither can our hair, without moisture our hair will break off very easily.

Think of your hair as set of scales with Moisture on one end and Protein on the other end, the aim is to keep the perfect balance of Moisture and Protein within your hair.

When we wash our hair it is saturated with water; as it dries we lose most of the water from our hair. The ideal amount of water to maintain within the cuticle is between 10 - 11%, this can be achieved by locking in the water by using an oil. As we know oil and water does not mix therefore the oil will create a barrier making it more difficult for the moisture to escape. For Natural hair heaver oils such as castor oil or olive oil are good natural oils to use. For a more technological designed product try *Sabino Moisture Block*; this is a great serum that seals in the moisture from water and makes the hair very resistant to water such a rain and sweat, and it washes out with regular shampooing.

Steam is another great way to get moisture into your hair. It can be as simple as wrapping a hot damp towel around your towel dried hair and securing it under a plastic cap. You could opt for a hooded hair steamer which may cost you a bit however it is a more efficient and effective way to get water into your hair, you can also sit and relax in the sauna or steam room for an intensive treatment.

Deep Conditioning
Deep Conditioning is the most effective way of drawing in the much needed moisture along with other important substances such as Amino Acids and Ceramides into the hair.

Many women of colour view deep conditioning as something that Afro hair does not need on a regular basis and when it is required on the odd occasion it has to be done by a professional in the form of a 'Treatment'.

Deep Conditioning does not have to be time consuming or expensive but it is extremely necessary if you want healthy hair that does not break off at the slightest touch. The process is fairly straight forward, after shampooing simply saturate your hair with a thick and creamy moisturising conditioner, it is wise to find one that is free of any proteins, you can either sit under a hooded steamer or hooded dryer with a plastic cap for half an hour if you do not have either of these you can simply sit with a plastic cap for two hours or as long as possible, for a really intensive treatment you can leave your deep conditioner in overnight. Aim to do this once a week to maintain healthy hair and twice a week for four weeks to nourish damaged hair.

Not all conditioners are designed to act as deep conditioners, look for a conditioner that suggest leaving on for 15 minutes or more, or an 'intensive treatment' or 'hair masque'. These are all clues that you are using a deep conditioner rather than a regular conditioner.

Co-Washing
Co-Washing is a term used for washing your hair with conditioner only. Washing your hair with shampoo several times a week can cause drying effects on your hair. However washing your hair several times a week with a 1-5 minute light inexpensive conditioner can dramatically improve its condition. Co-washing is great for Natural and Texturised hair as it brings fullness and definition back to the hair. Relaxed hair can also benefit from Co-washing; however it does make wearing straighter styles difficult. Simply rinse, comb the conditioner through the length of the hair avoiding your scalp and leave in for a few minutes then rinse out. When Co-washing it is best to leave your hair to dry naturally either free if you are Natural or in lose plaits, a bun or tied under a scarf.

Daily Moisturiser
You can top up your moisture levels throughout the day by using a daily moisturiser, these come in two forms; a spray liquid based moisturiser or cream based moisturiser. Apply these lightly all over the hair every morning and evening, these also help with freshening up a hair style. If you Co-wash there is less need to use a daily moisturiser.

A simple mixture that you can mix up at home that is very effective is 1 part vegetable glycerine, 1 part aloe vera gel and 4 parts water or rosewater; you can even add some essential oils for fragrance.

It is important not to go overboard with too much moisture in your hair. If you hair is over moisturised your hair will feel limp and mushy (think of paper left to sit in water). If you deep condition once or twice a week there is no need to co-wash your hair instead a light daily moisturiser will keep your hair well moisturised. If you co-wash several times a week or even daily then a deep condition may only be required once every 10 days. Well moisturised hair will feel cool to the touch when has been dried, hair that is lacking moisture will feel straw-like and rough and hair that is over moisturised will feel far too soft and mushy. This is why it is important to learn and understand what you hair needs.

2. PROTEIN

Our hair is made up of 88% of one basic Protein and that is Keratin, it is responsible for making our hair strong. As we manipulate our hair through heat styling and chemicals such as Relaxers; the Keratin in the hair is reduced.

Relaxed hair is more prone to protein loss as during the Relaxing process the protein bonds in the hair are broken and reformed therefore changing the texture of the hair; this is why protein treatments are vital to the health of Relaxed hair.

Products such as *Aphogee 2-Step Treatment for Damaged hair* or a *Brazilian Keratin Treatment* is ideal for severely damaged hair. This treatment is a heavy weight reconstructor; treatments like these must be followed with a very moisturising deep conditioner to restore the balance. You can opt for a more lightweight Protein conditioner or treatment spray if your hair is not severely damaged or awaiting a chemical process, these conditioners or leave-in treatments can be used on a weekly basis to maintain the strength in your hair. Silk proteins can also be very beneficial to the health of Afro hair; they provide the hair with shine and flexibility as well as providing a moderate level of heat protection. When buying any protein treatments look for ones that contain vegetable protein rather than animal protein as these are a similar match to Keratin that is naturally found within our own hair.

As you begin to understand your hair you will be able to tell what your hair is lacking, typically if your hair has too much protein your hair will feel dry and hard and will break more easily.

3. CERAMIDES

Ceramides are important oil-soluble compounds found within hair; they act as glue and are responsible for maintaining proper moisture and elasticity. Ceramides also create a natural barrier limiting moisture and protein loss and limiting the penetration of pollution and other harmful factors. When the hair is over processed from Relaxers or other chemical treatments the ceramides levels are depleted, causing hair to become dry, brittle and very fragile. Ceramides are used to maintain healthy hair rather than repairing damaged hair.

For Relaxer users ceramides are very important as they bind the hair together giving it flexibility and reducing breakage.

There are some great ceramide products out on the market such as *Matrix Biolage Cera-Repair Pro4* this is a concentrated treatment that conditions and strengthens the hair. Another great product that provides a good amount of Ceramide is *L'Oreal Elvive Damage Care 10X Ceramide Leave-In Concentrate* this is a nice lightweight leave-in conditioner that you can apply after every deep condition. Ceramides are also found naturally in some oils such as wheat germ oil, sunflower oil and hemp seed oil.

4. OILS

Oils are important in maintaining healthy Afro hair, they are important when locking in moisture, detangling and creating suppleness. Oils work by creating a barrier on your hair's surface locking in what moisture is within the hair shaft.

There are many 'miracle' formulas out there on the market aimed at black consumers, however many of them do more harm than good. Petroleum often called Mineral oil is a man made oil, this has negative effects on all hair types not just Afro, it clogs the pores preventing your scalp from breathing and it coats the hair preventing any nutrients from entering the hair. If you have a product that contains mineral oil (especially if it is the top three ingredients on the list) get rid of it!

There are many of other wonderful oils that you can use that are far better than any mineral oil. Oils such as jojoba, coconut, sweet almond and alma oils are light oils that are great for daily use or for Relaxed hair. If you are looking for heavier oils for Natural hair or to assist with styling; castor, olive and avocado oils are also very good. Aloe vera gel is a healthy alternative to traditional gels that contain alcohol which is very drying, this can be used to create sleek hair styles and tidy the hairline and nape.

Shea Butter is another great oil based product that can be used for just about anything, you can mix it with conditioners, apply it to damp hair before plaiting, apply to dry hair to tame fluffiness and it is great for skin care too. If you are going to use shea butter find a good quality unrefined organic grade, shea butter brought from local high street beauty chains tend to be filled with counterproductive chemicals and may contain mineral oil. You can find good quality shea butter from African stores and on many good organic and whole foods stores and websites.

Essential oils can be added to oils to enhance them even more, oils such a peppermint and tea tree oil can be added to create invigorating treatments that can be used on your hair or scalp. Test out some oils and see which ones are right for you.

Most oils do not moisture the hair they just sit on the hair sealing in what moisture is already in the hair; however coconut oil and olive oil do moisture the hair by 90% and 50%, castor oil is well known for thickening the hair shaft and grape seed oil is known to encourage hair growth.

5. PRE - SHAMPOO

Shampoo's work by stripping the grease and dirt from your hair, this often strips most of the natural moisture from the hair shaft too. Treating your hair with a conditioner or oil or both before you use shampoo can help protect and nourish the hair during washing. Apply the oil to the length and ends of your hair and allow it to sit on your hair under a plastic cap or warm towel for 30 minutes or more to achieve the most nourishing results.

6. CLARIFYING & CHELATING

The use of hair products and pollutants in the air from daily life can build up on the hair causing it to look dull and lifeless; this can create a barrier that can prevent moisture, protein and other essential ingredients from entering into the hair and preventing it from nourishing the hair shaft.

Regular shampoos are safe to use once or twice a week on Afro hair, any more and they will strip the hair of natural moisture. Not washing your hair enough will clog the follicles and weigh down the hair.

Sometimes regular shampoos are not enough and your hair may require more intense cleansing. A clarifying shampoo is used to eliminate product build up from the hair once a month.

Chelating shampoo's work deeper than clarifying shampoo's, not only do they remove surface build up but they also remove impurities from within the hair such as hard water, chlorine, minerals and medications. Chelating shampoo's cleanse the hair right down to the cortex therefore it is beneficial to use these one week before a chemical process such as Relaxers or Colour treatments to achieve a more even finish. A good chelating shampoo is *Paul Mitchell Three Shampoo*.

If you are a swimmer it is a good idea to thoroughly wet your hair before getting into chlorinated water, this will block a lot of the chlorine from entering your hair, but you will still need to follow up with a chelating shampoo and deep conditioner.

7. COLOUR

Colouring Afro hair; whether it is Relaxed or Natural takes a lot of preparation. It is not as simple as selecting colour you like then applying it. Your hair needs to be in tip top condition to safely colour your hair with either semi-permanent or permanent hair colour.

Hair dyes disrupt your hair's natural porosity level (how absorbent your hair is) making your hair more prone to moisture loss and breakage. This is why it is very important to prepare your hair with intensive protein, moisturising treatments and trims prior to colouring your hair. Colouring damaged hair i.e. hair that is excessively breaking or shedding can cause serious problems and the colour may come out far different than expected.

It is possible to successfully colour Relaxed hair however you must wait at least 2 weeks AFTER you Relax your hair to colour it. As Relaxers are the stronger chemical out of the two therefore you need this time in between to rebuild the strength and condition of your hair, as the common saying is that you "Colour a Relaxer, not Relax a Colour".

Use a good chelating shampoo to remove any mineral deposits prior to colouring your hair to achieve a more even colour. Follow this up with a moisture and protein conditioner such as *Organic Root Stimulator Replenishing Conditioner.*

When deciding on a hair colour; specialist hair colourists suggest going 1 or 2 shades either side of your natural colour. If you are looking for a more drastic change then go to a professional hair colour specialist.

When applying the colour to achieve intensive vibrant results, sit under a hooded dryer with a medium heat, this will allow the colour to penetrate further into the hair shaft making the colour richer and more long lasting, wait for the hair to cool down before rinsing out the dye with cool water.

Henna is a great alternative to using traditional hair dyes. Henna is a natural plant based dye that is mixed with different substances such as coffee to alter the colour. Colouring your hair with Henna can improve the condition of your hair and colourless Henna can be used alone as a conditioner. You can layer Henna on by applying it every day for 3 days this will give long lasting and vibrant results, the colour you achieve from using Henna can last anywhere from a few months to a year depending on the intensity you apply it at during the application time. *Lush* do a range of Henna dyes that are of a high quality and easy to use. After you have successfully coloured your hair you want to keep vibrant for as long as possible. Wait at least 2-3 days after colouring your hair to wash it again, washing your hair will cause you to lose a bit of your colour each time. After the first week washing once a week with cool water is fine for colour treated hair alternating with moisture and protein deep conditioners.

Avoid the over use of heat styling as this will draw the colour out from your hair. Hard water and chlorinated water can strip your hair colour; try using a chelating shampoo once a month to deep cleanse the hair shaft and remove any chlorine.

Avoid going outdoors with damp colour treated hair as harsh conditions and sunlight all assist in stripping your hair of its new colour. Look for products that are especially designed for colour treated hair, their complex formulas help to lock in the colour making your colour last for as long as possible. Steer clear of products containing alcohol as these strip the colour from your hair.

If permanently colouring your hair is too much of a big step for you; then try experimenting with coloured clip in section or have some coloured hair woven in with your own hair, you can choose natural subtle colours as high and low lights or opt for bright vivid colours for a more daring look.

8. HEAT

When using heat on Afro hair it is important not to overdo it. Heat is extremely damaging to Afro hair whether it is Relaxed or Natural. As Afro hair is very dry the heat draws out what little moisture the hair can retain thereby causing the hair to be overly dry and break very easily.

Using heat for styling purposes can be effective and not cause much breakage if done correctly. If you like to wear your hair straight on a weekly basis then try allowing your hair to dry naturally for a few hours, to achieve a more smoother finish tie your hair back in a loose bun on several loose plaits or twists. Once your hair is completely dry you can use a ceramic or tourmaline straightening iron to get the straight sleek look. Ceramic and Tourmaline irons are the best for all hair types as they glide along the hair shaft and do not drag the cuticles.

Some people prefer to blow dry their hair, this can be damaging if the proper tools are not used. Round brushes, comb attachments and tension are all very well for European hair but on Afro hair this can cause severe damage and aggravation of the cuticle and over time can lead to breakage. If you do opt for a hand held blow dryer use a large cushioned paddle brush along with a seamless wide toothed comb to detangle and distribute the heat without ripping out and damaging your hair.

An ideal way to use heat to assist in drying is by using a hooded dryer on a low to medium heat setting, sectioning your hair in small sections and wrapping it around large smooth rollers. The roller method allows your hair to dry straight with plenty of bounce and body. The ends of your hair will lay nice and smooth but with some curls, these can be brushed out and if you wrap your hair for up to an hour you can achieve a very sleek look that lasts a lot longer than using ceramic irons and is far more kinder to your hair. Whichever method you use always use a heat protectant on your hair before using heat on it.

9. POROSITY

Porosity is used to measure how much moisture your hair absorbs. Porosity is measured in low, medium and high. The more compact your cuticle is (i.e. the more overlapping cells your cuticle has) the harder it is for moisture to penetrate and escape from your hair, the less compact your cuticle cells are the easier it is for moisture to transfer.

Hair that has low porosity is more resistant to Relaxers, Colour treatments and Deep Conditioners. Low

Porosity hair takes longer to dry and to fully saturate with water, this can often mean that the hair holds too much moisture and not enough protein. On the other hand high Porosity hair is the exact opposite and is overly dry which leads to excessive breaking and shedding.

Porosity levels can be balanced by using acid-balanced conditioning treatments such as *Roux Porosity Control Conditioner* or a mixture of apple cider vinegar and water to bring the pH level down to a normal level of 4.5 - 5.5 and regulating the cuticle layer which in turn locks-in moisture on overly-porous / low porosity hair, this also helps to remove any residue from products creating a clean silky finish for styling.

10. SCALP

A healthy scalp is very important in the health and growth of your hair, think of your scalp as an extension of your face, applying too many heavy and harmful oils to the scalp will clog the pores just as it would on your face, this leads to excessive drying and dandruff as the scalp is starved of the essential natural moisture that it craves. I am sure you remember as a child sitting on the floor as your mother greased your scalp and plaited your hair. This was usually to combat dry looking scalps and add shine to the hair. But is greasing the scalp really necessary? The answer is No, in fact greasing the scalp with products such as *Blue Grease, Pink Oil Moisturiser* and *Vaseline* do far more harm than good, as they contain Petroleum also referred to as Mineral oil which clogs the pores in the scalp and coat the hair shaft starving it of receiving moisture.

The hair; even Afro hair is very good at creating its own natural oils, there is often no need for any additional oil on the scalp, with regular washing and deep conditioning your scalp will be able to regulate itself. If however you find your scalp feeling tight or dry then you can opt for using natural plant based oil on your scalp. A great alternative to the traditional grease is coconut oil, the texture and consistency of coconut oil is very similar to grease when kept at room temperature, coconut oil is the only natural oil that penetrates into the hair shaft by 90% as well as providing the shine and calming itchy scalps, this is superb as no 'grease' could ever come that close to providing that much nourishment. Try applying the coconut oil thinly in sections of hair two times a week when your scalp is feeling overly dry, massaging it into your scalp will stimulate the hair follicles encouraging new growth, adding a few drops of pure tea tree oil will leave your scalp feeling cool and tingling and calm any itchiness.

Other factors that can also irritate the scalp are extreme or excessive heat, harsh products and tension, these can all contribute to an unhealthy scalp with in turn will lead to unhealthy hair.

GROWING YOUR HAIR

CARING FOR YOUR ENDS

As women of colour we face tougher obstacles when trying to grow long healthy hair whether it is Natural, Relaxed or Texturised. Afro hair has difficulties holding onto moisture which in turn leads to breakage, breakage makes it very difficult for hair to retain length and grow even longer.

In order to minimise breakage and retain length it is important to make sure the ends of your hair are well cared for this means ensuring that they are well moisturised, trimmed and free of split ends regularly.

Wearing your hair out on a daily basis when trying to grow your hair is not a good idea as your hair can rub on your clothes or accessories causing the ends of your hair to break and become damaged, if this happens it will be very difficult for your hair to reach beyond the length of the damage; usually shoulder length.

You can ensure the ends of your hair are in the best condition they can be by checking them regularly for split ends; trimming off a few millimeters at a time (often called Dusting) can help reduce split ends and the need for more drastic trimming or cutting. Applying extra moisture on the ends of your at night is another way of giving your hair some extra care, a good method is applying a moisturising conditioner such as *Aubrey Organics Honeysuckle and Rose Moisturising conditioner* on the ends of the hair followed by coconut oil to seal it in, your hair will feel soft and moisturised in the morning.

PROTECTIVE STYLES

When trying to grow your hair to longer lengths try to style your hair in a way that the ends of your hair are protected especially if your hair sits at your shoulders. You can try wearing your hair in a bun and tucking the ends of your hair right under, this can be jazzed up by teaming it with a sophisticated swooping side fringe and a cute clip. If your hair is too short to put in a bun you can try a clip on ponytail or bun, these secure by using built in combs and drawstrings to hold it in place. Clip on ponytails and buns are great for damaged hair as you can treat your hair to an intensive deep conditioning treatment by slathering the ends of your own hair underneath the clip on with a creamy conditioner and oil mixture then cover with a small clear plastic bag or cling film to keep the conditioner from drying out and adding heat for greater penetration, no one will ever know the difference as it will be hidden.

Other great alternatives are to wear weaves, wigs or half wigs (I will go more into this in a later chapter). I prefer half wigs over full wigs and weaves; this is because they are easier to maintain your own hair underneath, you can wash and condition your hair on a weekly basis.

DETANGLING

When detangling Afro hair it is important that care is taken and the right tools are used. Dry hair is far stronger than wet hair. When combing Natural hair; section your hair in 8 sections and start combing from the ends working your way up your hair using a wide toothed comb such as a *K-Cutter comb* which is great for Natural hair, even though the hair is more fragile wet Natural hair responded best when wet and saturated with a conditioner to provide slip and prevent snagging, *Jilbere shower combs* are good for combing wet hair regardless of the texture you can follow this up with a *Denman D3 or D4* brush to remove every last knot.

Relaxed hair tangles less than Natural hair so a regular wide toothed comb followed by a Denman brush on dry hair will be sufficient to detangle the hair, fine rattail combs should never be used to detangle Relaxed hair, these are designed for 1 hair types and will cause breakage, again start from the ends and work your way up sectioning the hair in 2 – 4 sections, again a Jilbere shower comb or a seam free wide toothed comb is the best tool to use when combing wet hair and distributing conditioner.

A healthy scalp needs a constant supply of blood circulation to do its job properly. If your scalp is healthy with good blood circulation your hair will also be healthy. Scalp massages assist in bringing these much needed nutrients from the blood to the scalp.

HAIR STIMULATORS

Scalp massages can be used for stress relief as well as scalp stimulants, they also enable proper distribution of sebum across your scalp which helps to protect your scalp from the daily elements and dryness. Scalp massages can help to speed up hair growth in thinning areas by redirecting nutrients to where they are most needed.

Hair grows at a rate of half an inch per month; there are products on the market that aim to increase the natural growth rate.

Products such as *Mega Tek, Ovation Cell Therapy* and *Nexxus Vitatress Biotin Crème* all aim to promote an increase in hair grown between 10 – 50%, they work by stimulating the hair follicle and encouraging growth, these products also help the new hair to emerge stronger from the follicle therefore leading to less breakage as the hair grows.

If you do not like the idea of using an artificial product to increase hair growth you can try mixing several essential oils together. Try mixing thyme and atlas cedarwood essential oils (2 drops), lavender and rosemary (3 drops) essential oils with half a teaspoon of jojoba oil and 4 teaspoons of grapeseed oil to create a refreshing stimulating hair growth oil. Whichever method you choose (if any) ensure you massage it in thoroughly for 5 - 10 minutes for maximum effect.

ARTIFICIAL HAIR

HUMAN HAIR V'S SYNTHETIC HAIR

Synthetic hair and Human hair can both be used to create a natural looking style. Human hair is hair taken directly off a human head. The most common hair used for weaves and extensions within the Afro hair industry is Asian hair, European hair is used also however the individual strands tend to be finer than Asian strands which are better suited to Afro hair.

Human hair is very versatile and manageable, but to get the most out of your purchase you have to treat it with as much care as you would your own hair, this means refrain from using excessive heat, wash regularly with plenty of deep conditioning. Synthetic hair cannot be exposed to heat such as curling irons, hair straighteners and blow dryers. As Synthetic hair is made up of fine plastic strands; any heat will cause the hair to melt. Synthetic hair can last up to 3 months before it starts to become very tangled and knotty. Human hair can last for over a year with good maintenance. Synthetic hair should be maintained as best as it can by washing it weekly in cool water with a mild shampoo and allowing it to air dry naturally, and should not be combed when wet especially if the hair is curly, the curls may drop somewhat but once the hair is dry it will spring back to its original shape. Spraying your Synthetic hair daily with a braid spray will ensure it does not get too many tangles and retains a healthy natural looking shine.

WEAVES

Weaves are the most popular method of wearing artificial hair amongst women of colour. They are very versatile and offer the wearer freedom of styles. There are 2 types of methods of installing weaves, the first is by gluing rows of hair onto clean; oil free hair. This will last for approximately two weeks however this type of glue is extremely damaging to your own hair underneath. The second and far more healthier method is get a sew-in weave; where rows of hair are sewn onto canerowed hair, this will last up to 2 months with proper care.

In order to make your weave last and look the most natural it is advisable to use good quality Human hair, using synthetic hair will cause your style to look matted and untidy in a matter of weeks, unlike wigs weaves do not have the flexibility to be changed as frequently or taken off at night. Look after your weave by detangling it daily and using a spray formulated for artificial hair, washing it weekly and conditioning it after every wash. It is important to look after your own hair whilst wearing a weave. Start by diluting a moisturising shampoo with water and applying it directing to the canerows; section at a time; this will ensure that your hair is clean and free of any build up, deep condition your canerows by slathering on conditioner directly to the area and leave it to sit for an hour, rinse out thoroughly and allow your hair to dry thoroughly under a hooded hair dryer.

When removing a weave; time and patience is required, if the hair is not to tangled unpick the stitching and unravel the canerow section at a time, if the hair is tangled spray the hair with a leave-in conditioner or apply regular conditioner to the canerow, this will help the plaits unravel very easily. Ensure you thoroughly detangle your hair before shampooing it, as wetting your hair if it is knotty will cause your hair to lock and it will be very difficult to comb out. After washing treat your hair to a protein treatment or conditioner followed by a moisturising conditioner then a leave-in conditioner or moisturising oil such as coconut oil.

Wait at least a week before attempting to Relax or Colour your hair as your hair will need some time to recover, you can use this time to experiment with styles such as canerows or trying out a wig or a clip on ponytail.

BRAIDS

Braid maintenance should be treated exactly the same as sew-in weaves, in order for your braids look shiny and tidy moisturise your braids regularly and seal using a thick oil such as castor oil or shea butter.

Never burn off excess hair that may stick out of your braids as this is your own hair and will cause damage. At night secure your braids in one or 2 large plaits to prevent them from tangling at night. With good maintenance and good quality Human hair your braids should last up to three months.

WIGS

Wigs are becoming more a more popular than they were in past years. The styles and quality of wigs have improved dramatically so much so that more and more women are opting for wigs over weaves. Wigs offer a great advantage over weaves as you can properly wash, condition and care for your own hair. There are two types of wigs available, full wigs, these cover the whole of the head and usually have some sort of fringe in the front, they are secured by a series of combs or straps to hold the wig in place. Lace front wigs, often worn by some celebrities are the most natural looking wigs available on the market and can set you back £500 or more. These offer a very natural look as each hair is individually sewn onto lace offering a very natural looking hairline.

Half wigs start further back on the head; these give the wearer the added convenience of blending her own hair with the hair on the wig to provide a natural looking style.

To preserve the quality of the wig whether it is Human or Synthetic hair it should not be slept in over night as this damages the fibres and strands of the hair. Wigs should be washed once or twice a week in a mild shampoo in luke warm water and conditioner should be applied to the wig for 5 minutes, if the wig is human hair you can comb the conditioner through to remove any tangles, for Synthetic hair detangle the wig thoroughly with a Denman brush BEFORE you wet it.

CREATING YOUR OWN HAIR CARE REGIME

Taking the health of your hair into your own hands can be very empowering and exciting yet somewhat confusing. Deciphering between all of the new information can be difficult to comprehend, as each head is different the same regime may not be suitable for everyone even if they do have the same hair type.

This section will give you a detailed review of what you will need and how and when to use them.

1. Moisturising Shampoo
This should be used once or twice a week, usually one lathering should be enough unless your hair has a lot of build up.

Examples: Crème of Nature (red and green label) Shampoo, Neutrogena Triple Moisture Cream Lather Shampoo, Aveda Sap Moss Shampoo and Elasta QP crème conditioning shampoo, Aphogee Moisturising Shampoo.

2. Clarifying or Chelating Shampoo
These should be used once a month, your hair will feel squeaky clean after using these shampoos. They should also be used one week before a chemical treatment such as a Relaxer or Colour application so time your usage carefully.

Examples: Kenra Clarifying Shampoo, Pantene Pro-V Purity Shampoo, Shampoo Three' by Paul Mitchell, Aveda Detox, Nexxus Aloe Rid Shampoo,

3. Moisturising Deep Conditioner
This should be used after every wash and should be left on the hair for 30 minutes under a hooded dryer or 2 hours under a plastic cap without heat. A moisturising deep conditioner only needs to be used once a week, if you wash your hair more than once a week the second wash can be followed with a light 10

minute condition. The majority of the time that you condition your hair will be with a moisturising conditioner however sometimes you will need to use a protein conditioner. 1 in 4 times you condition should be with a protein conditioner.

Examples: Keracare Humecto, Aubrey Organics, Crème of Nature Nourishing Conditioner, Neutrogena Triple Moisture Daily Conditioner, Elasta QP DPR-11, Organic Root Stimulator Replenishing Pak.

4. Protein Treatments

These are used for rebuilding damage to the hair. The condition of your hair will determine how often protein is needed in your regime. There are different levels of intensity with protein. Light protein conditioners can be used every 2-3 weeks for touch ups to keep your levels maintained. Heavy treatments should be used prior to a chemical service or to correct severely damaged hair and should always be followed with a moisturising deep conditioner. Relaxed hair requires more protein than Natural hair, Natural hair can use light protein every 2 weeks but rarely need heavy protein treatments.

Examples: Light Conditioner
Aphogee 2 Minute Keratin Reconstructor, Aubrey Organics GPB, Joico K-Pac.

Examples: Heavy Treatment
Aphogee Treatment for Damaged Hair, Dudley's DRC, Nexxus Emergencée Strengthening Polymeric Reconstructor.

5. Leave-in Conditioner

A water based moisturising leave-in conditioner should be used after every wash, and can also be used as a daily moisturiser once in the morning and once and night. Protein leave-in conditioners should be used once a week or as needed or when using heat to style.

Examples: Moisture
Neutrogena Triple Moisture Silk Touch Leave-in, VO5 Miracle Mist Leave-in, Aussie Miracle Hair Insurance Leave-in.

Examples: Protein
Aphogee Keratin & Green Tea Restructuriser, CHI Keratin Mist, Elasta QP Oil Recovery Moisturiser

6. Natural Oils

These oils are used for sealing in moisture, they also aid in improving the pliability of the hair and adding shine. By starting at the ends and working your way up the hair shaft will ensure that then ends are fully coated without weighing down the length of hair.

Examples: Coconut oil, Olive oil, Avocado oil, Almond oil, Jojoba oil, Sweet Almond oil, Carrot oil, Castor oil, Vatika oil, Alma oil, Shea Butter.

7. Essential Oils (optional)

These are wonderful scalp stimulants. These must be mixed with heavier, carrier oil because they are extremely potent. Only use a few drops per application. Essential oils can also be added to conditioners, moisturisers, leave-ins, and shampoos. They are great for scalp massages, and very regimen friendly

Examples: Lavender, Rosemary, Peppermint, Tea Tree, Thyme, Ylang Ylang, Lavender, Cedar Wood

8. Other hair tools:

Satin Scarf, Bonnet, and or Satin Pillowcases
Wide and medium toothed seamless comb
A boar or soft bristle brush
Hair pins/clips
Rollers
Plastic Shower Caps
A pair of hair scissors
A detangling brush

The more you experiment with good products and techniques the more you will learn and understand your hair, take time to observe how products work and how your hair reacts at different times of the day/week/month. Some people who are just starting on their hair care journey find it helpful to keep a hair diary. Write down how your hair reacts, what products you like, what you don't like, what you are interested in purchasing and what hairstyles you like, you can start off in the 'Notes' section in the back!

Hair care should be fun and not a chore, so work with what you have and enjoy it!

CHILDREN'S HAIR CARE

Children's hair care should be very simple and gentle. Excessive combing and tugging will aggravate the scalp and cause breakage. Try simple canerows, braids or a few ponytails decorated with one or 2 hair accessories any more than this will weighing the hair down and can create tension giving your little ones a sore head.

Create a simple regime by washing the hair once a week with a mild baby shampoo or natural shampoo such as *Aubrey Organics Honey Suckle and Rose Moisturising shampoo*. In their very early years conditioner is not always required as children's hair creates a lot of its own natural moisture, follow up with sealing in the moisture with a light oil such as coconut or jojoba oil or even a leave-in conditioner formulated for curly hair that is free of petroleum.

When using products on young Afro hair it is far better to opt for organic natural products or even make your own products. Using a blend coconut oil, shea butter, essential oils, other natural oils and vegetable glycerine, which are very easily obtained from health stores and online. Try creating a mixture that moisturises and defines the curls of your child's hair by using some of your favorite ingredients.

As children's hair texture is always changing it is harmful to use any chemicals such as Relaxers and Colour treatments on such fragile hair. Relaxers can have such damaging effects on adult hair if not used properly and have the potential to damage such young hair by causing severe breakage and dryness and sores to the scalp.

Children are very easily influenced and the use of Relaxers and or hair extensions including braids, weaves and wigs often cause young children to believe that their natural Afro hair is not something that they should be proud of instead it can be interpreted as something that they should hide. The book, *Nappy Hair; by Carolivia Herron* is a fantastic book and encourages young children of colour to embraces their unique Afro hair type.

SKIN CARE

SKIN TYPES

NORMAL SKIN

Normal skin is often the most desired skin type. It is smooth and evenly toned in texture and it does not often experience breakouts, the pores are small and not easily visible. The skins balance of oil and moisture is consistent and this allows the skin to glow with a soft velvety finish. To keep normal skin looking its best it is important to have a good skin care regime.

OILY SKIN

Oily skin can be somewhat difficult to manage. Oily skin has over reactive sebaceous glands; which makes the skin appear shiny and feel greasy especially over the T-zone (the forehead, nose and chin area). The pores on oily skin become enlarged; which makes the skin more prone to acne and blemishes.

Oily skin needs sufficient cleansing in order to keep the pores from becoming clogged and blocked which will lead to black-heads and spots.

DRY SKIN

Dry skin lacks natural oil and moisture, it chaps and flakes easily and appears patchy, fragile and thin. Dry skin can crease very easily and soaks up whatever moisture is applied to it. The pores on dry skin are practically invisible and blackheads and acne are not very common.

COMBINATION SKIN

Combination skin is rather difficult to manage as it requires separate treatments for each area. Combination skin is often oily along the T-zone area and dry across the cheeks. Regular cleansing, toning and moisturising have to be done on those difficult areas. Cleanse and tone the oily patches and apply extra moisture to the dry areas.

SENSITIVE SKIN

Sensitive skin can fluctuate due to internal and external changes. Sensitive skin can be dry, oily or combination although somewhat exaggerated and is easily disrupted by harsh products. Sensitive skin is often blotchy and often has broken veins. Sensitive skin may be so sensitive that you may need to consult a Dermatologist which will be able to help you balance your skin.

DAILY REGIMES

CLEANSERS

Cleansing your skin is the first step in your skin care regime, how you choose to cleanse your skin will depend on your skin type. Choose what method of cleanser you prefer; thick frothy facial washes are great for Oily skin; *Origins Checks and Balance* or *Origins Get Down* facial washes are both marvellous. Normal skins are best suited to gel cleansers where as Dry skin responds well to cream wipe off cleansers.

Oil based cleansers are a great alternative for all skin types particularly dry and oily skin types. We have all heard the saying that oil and water does not mix, the same applies to skin care. As oil secretes from our skin most water based cleansers cannot remove it sufficiently instead the oil is moved round the skin from one area to another. As like attracts like, oil from your skin will be attracted to a natural oil you put onto your skin sort of like a magnet, it can then be removed from the skin by using a hot damp facecloth.

This works by applying a mixture of 60% castor oil and 40% olive oil or jojoba oil (for sensitive eyes) to the skin, thoroughly covering the face and neck with plenty of the oil mixture, massage in the mixture for 2-3 minutes then take a clean face cloth and soak it in hot water; wring it out and allow it to sit on your face until it begins to cool. Now wipe away the oil and re dampen the cloth in hot water ensuring all of the oil is removed, you can repeat this process if necessary. For most people their skin will feel cleansed and nourished with no need for an additional moisturiser; however if your skin feels a little tight then you can apply a dab of oil or moisturiser to the skin. You can adjust the mixture to suit your skin type, more olive or jojoba oil will be more moisturising where as more castor oil will be more cleansing.

Brushes are a great way to boost your regular cleanser whilst giving your skin a gentle exfoliation treatment. There are some good hand held manual brushes from beauty companies such as *Dermalogica*, the holy grail of deep cleansing facial brushes is the luxurious *Clarisonic Sonic Skin Cleansing Systems*. This works by using a patented sonic frequency of more than 300 movements per second to clean, soften and smooth your skin. They remove six time more make-up and dirt than regular washing and leave the skin smoother allowing the skin to absorb products more effectively.

TONERS

Toners are used after cleansing to remove any traces of dirt or make-up that may be left behind as well as tightening pores and balancing the pH of your skin. These days the use of toners is not essential to your skin care regime as most cleansers no longer leave behind that residue and the pH levels in cleansers are not as harsh as they used to be. Many toners contain alcohol however these ones tend to dry the skin out causing skin problems such as dryness or greasiness skin as the pores have to work overtime to put back what the alcohol has stripped away. Some great alcohol free toners are *United State, Make A Difference* and *Oil Refiner* all from *Origins* and *Neutrogena Alcohol Free Toner* all really improve the texture and feel of your skin after washing.

There are some natural toners that are good alternative to regular alcohol based toners, you can try Rosewater or distilled witch hazel, this is good for normal, dry and sensitive skin or oily and combination skins can benefit from using a mixture of 50% apple cider vinegar and 50% water this works very well for fading marks and giving an even looking complexion the scent of the vinegar can be quite strong but this will disappear as the mixture dries.

MOISTURISERS

When choosing a moisturiser it is important that you find one that feels great, one that does not leave your skin greasy and also smells pleasant too. A good moisturiser should never irritate your skin or eyes. As moisture is water it is a good idea to apply your moisturiser to damp skin, this helps to lock in some additional moisture that you would have lost out on.

Choose a moisturiser that is designed especially for your skin type and age, if you suffer with acne, spot fighting formulas are best for you or you can add a few drops of pure tea tree oil to your favorite moisturiser. Oily skin should opt for oil free and matifying moisturisers such as *Lancôme Pure Focus Lotion Matifying Moisturizing Lotion Oil-Free.* Dry skin needs something richer; a good store brought moisturiser is *Clarins Super*

Restorative Day Cream For Very Dry Skin or you can opt for a natural oil such as avocado oil which is very moisturising or Shea butter which is perfect for black skin; remember a little goes a long way. It is important for Sensitive skin to use products that have little to no unnecessary chemicals. Brands such as *Aveno* and *Aubrey Organics* and *Origins* do good products that are kinder to sensitive skins.

All skin needs to use a daily moisturiser with an SPF; even black skin, an SPF of 15 is suitable for most skin except for the very pale who would need to go up to SPF30+. In sunnier conditions you will need to up your SPF from 15 to 30 to accommodate for the more intense UV rays.

NIGHT CREAMS

As you sleep your skin transforms its primary function of protection to one of its other 15 functions of repairing and renewing itself. Many people believe that the use of a specialist night time moisturiser is a must in order to aid the skin. However the skin is a very complex organ and does not often need assistance. At night the skin 'breathes' and expels the waste it has attracted during the day; this is often why you may notice the odd spot or too after a night out as your skin has pushed out any pollutants that were trapped under it.

The use of heavy night creams often trap what your skin is trying to get rid of meaning your skin can never truly repair or renew itself to its full potential if it is being hindered. So what can you do to help your skin? Do nothing; yes that's right apply nothing to your skin at night instead after cleansing go to sleep with a bare face, it might feel strange and tight at first but as time goes on your skin will be used to its own environment again and begin to lubricate itself where it is needed.

If sleeping bare faced is too much of a shock to your system then try weaning yourself off of heavy night creams start of by using a fairly light night time moisturiser such as *Neutrogena Light Night Cream* then take it down to the next step by using a natural oil such as coconut oil which has high absorbent rate and is full of antioxidants that fight free radicals. Once you are comfortable using a light oil you should be at the stage where you can comfortably sleep bare faced.

TREATMENTS

FACE MASKS

Face masks are a must for a clear complexion; they are great at absorbing excess oil and refining larger pores. Use a face mask formulated for your skin type, masks containing clay; particularly Kaolin or Kea Kelp powder are great for oily skin and over oily T-zones *Origins Clear Improvement* is a great oil absorbing mask. Masks containing honey extracts are wonderful for dry and sensitive skins.

Steaming your face after cleansing and before applying your face mask opens the pores and draws out any impurities to the surface making it easier for your face mask to do the rest of the hard work. To make steaming more beneficial you can add a tablespoon of herbs to the water. Herbs like lavender, thyme and rosemary can be used as stimulants while cleansing.

There are many variations of masks that you can make at home; theses are a cheap and effective way of being sure you know exactly what you are putting onto your skin. Here are some examples of what you can use for your skin type. Mix the ingredients together to form a thick paste and apply the mask to clean skin and leave to sit for 10 - 15 minutes, wash off with warm water and pat your skin dry.

Normal Skin
Oatmeal and yoghurt mask, Egg whites and plain yoghurt mask,

Dry Skin
Milk and Honey mask

Oily Skin
French green clay, water and Honey mask, Ripe Banana, Orange and honey mask.

Sensitive Skin
Fuller's Earth clay, water and Honey mask,

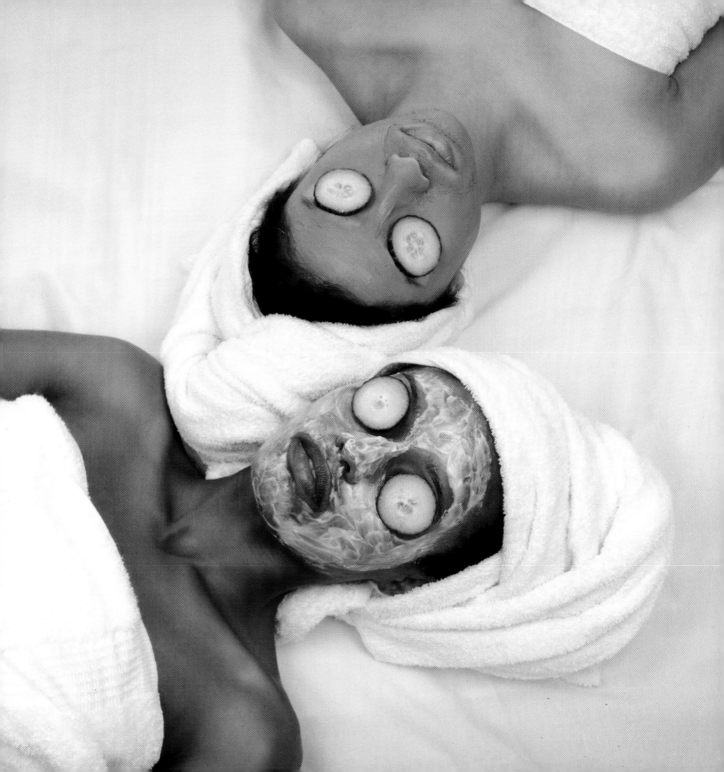

EXFOLIATORS

Exfoliation is very a important part of a good skincare routine and should be performed on a regular basis. Our skin is always regenerating and renewing itself and sometimes dead skin cells can sit on the surface and become trapped. As well as removing the dead skin cells, exfoliation helps detoxifying the skin, improves blood and lymph circulation and decreases dark circles under the eyes and calms the nervous system.

Exfoliation is usually performed with abrasive substances or complex acidic formulas that are able to clear the pores that become clogged with grease and dirt. These eliminate the dead cells from our skin leaving a fresher looking complexion.

Manual exfoliators can be made with natural substances such as sugar, baking soda and muslin cloths. Alternatively there are many great exfoliators such as *MAC Volcanic Ash Exfoliator, Estee Lauder Soft Clean Moisture Rich Exfoliator* or *Clinique Exfoliating Scrub.* Look for scrubs that are fairly fine in texture and dissolves easily, the texture should be similar to fine salt rather than grains of sand, products such as *St Ives Apricot Scrub* is far too abrasive for the face and should be used as a body exfoliator instead.

Another safe and very efficient method of exfoliation is chemical exfoliation. This type of exfoliation is performed by using chemical substances called hydroxy acids. These acids work by dissolving the intercellular cells 'glue' that 'sticks' the cells to the surface of the skin.

Glycoic, Lactic and Salicylic acids are hydroxy acids that are extremely effective on shedding dead cells. They are usually contained in all kinds of cosmetic creams, abrasives and exfoliating masks. Out of these three, Glycolic acid is the most powerful and usually causes some skin irritations, which is why it is not as highly recommended.

Exfoliation does not have to be intense, aim to exfoliate once or twice a week and with a very gentle formula. Over use of any exfoliant can cause sensitivity, blemishes and premature aging. Be sure to exfoliate clean skin and again steam will assist in the exfoliator to work at its best, rinse the face in cool to cold water to prevent irritation and to help close the pores.

CHEMICAL PEELS

A Chemical peel is a treatment is used to remove dead skin cells in order to reveal a fresher youthful looking completion. They are used to treat Acne scarring, fine lines and wrinkles, Hyperpigmentation and rough patchy skin. Although there are some good at home treatments, chemical peels are always best performed by a qualified Beautician or Dermatologist. Chemical Peels use an acidic formula that has a pH balance that is lower than the pH of your skin's natural pH.

Chemical peels are applied to skin that has been cleansed with a special substance and then begins to eat away at the intercellular cells that hold the skin together. Over the following 24 hours after a chemical peel the skin will appear red and swollen and some may experience a burning sensation. Over the next few days the skin will turn to a thick leathery texture as the skin starts to dry out, during this stage the skin must be well moisturised to prevent cracking which can lead to infections.

By day five the skin should be begin to peel away, it is important not to pick at the skin but instead let the skin shed at its own rate. As the skin heals you will see fresh new skin beginning to emerge, this skin will be sensitive for a week or so but you can wash and apply make-up normally just be careful not to aggravate or be too harsh with the new skin. Some people may experience a second round of shedding but not as excessive as the initial round, again this needs to be well moisturised however you can assist the shedding by taking a clean soft wash cloth and warm water to remove the flaky skin.

In the months after a chemical peel is extremely important to use a sunscreen every day as the skin will be very sensitive to light conditions and sun damage. Chemical peels are not just a one time treatment, these work best if used in a course of 6 - 8 treatments of at least three month intervals.

An alternative to Chemical Peels are natural peels that you can do at home with ingredients straight from your kitchen cupboard. Using ingredients such as apples, aspirin, berries, buttermilk, cherries, sour cream, grapefruit, grapes, lemon, lime, orange, pears, pineapple, papaya, raspberry, strawberries, sugar beets sugar, sugar cane sugar, tomato, wine, willow bark extract and yogurt.

Simply mash the fruit you have chosen and apply it to your face, you can also use a packet of unflavored gelatine to hold the mixture together and to create the mask effect that will allow you to peel off the mixture once it has dried on your skin. Allow the mixture to sit on your face for 30 minutes then rinse off.

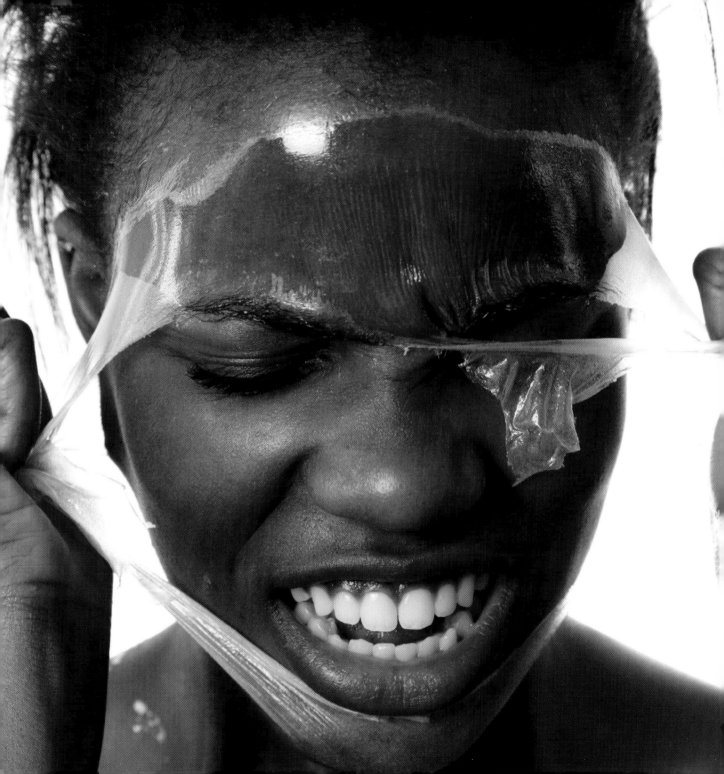

MAKE UP
PRIMERS & FOUNDATIONS

Primers are relatively new to the cosmetic market, they are transparent gel like formulas that you apply to clean moisturised skin, these create a barrier between your skin and the foundation and allows your foundation to go on more smoothly, last longer, absorb excess oils and also helps to minimise pores. One of the most recommended foundation primers on the market is the *Smashbox Photo Finish Foundation Primer SPF 15*.

The perfect foundation should match your skin tone exactly, the whole point to wearing foundation is to make your skin look flawless and polished not to appear darker or lighter, your foundation should disappear into your skin and blend with your jaw line, however this is easier said than done.

When shopping for a foundation it is a good idea to go with a clean moisturised face. Choose colours that are similar to your skin and test them out on your jaw line, the ones that you can hardly see requires a second look in natural daylight, take a small handheld mirror with you and take a look at the colours outside as daylight is what most people will see you in the majority of the time.

Most black skins have red, yellow and golden under tones so stick to brands which have a large range of darker tones such as *MAC, Make-up Forever* and *Bare Essentials*. Steer clear of high street brands that tend to only have one or two darker shades as these tend to use pink undertones which leave black skins looking grey and ashy. A real investment foundation is to get one created especially for you, *Prescriptives* do a custom range where you can decided on a variety of coverage's and special ingredients such as oil absorbing or extra moisture. Another good custom range is *Colorlab Cosmetics* which is a brand from USA that is sold in some high end department stores.

Foundation is best applied with a foundation brush using circular motions in the direction of your hair growth, take time to really buff in the product into your skin to create a natural looking finish. Applying concealer the same colour as your foundation right under your eyes can really bring a youthful look to the face, look up into a mirror and whatever areas looks darker under your eye apply the concealer using a concealer brush, gently blend the concealer in using your ring finger then gently blend again with the foundation brush to create a seamless join. The concealer should be applied to the bare skin here and not over the foundation as it will look too heavy and age the eye area.   When using concealer to hide blemishes; apply it after the foundation otherwise the foundation will just wipe it away.

If you are lucky enough to have next to flawless skin you might want to try a tinted moisturiser or concealer to touch up the odd one or two blemishes that you might have; *Kevyn Aucoin The Sensual Skin Enhancer* is a fantastic concealer that gives you a flawless finish but requires a lot of blending for a really natural finish. A great tinted moisturiser is *Smashbox Sheer Focus Tined Moisturiser*, follow this up with a light dusting of loose powder or oil control powder will seal your base making it ready for your next step.

BLUSHERS & BRONZERS

Many darker skinned women often skip the use of blushers as they find it unnecessary and reserved only for fairer skins, but this is not the case. There are many shades of blushers suitable for all women from the very pale to the very dark; it's just a matter of selecting the right shade for you.

Blushers are best applied to the apples of your cheeks in a soft gentle motion, gone are the days when you applied blusher in a diagonal line up towards your hairline.

Blushers come in several consistencies, the traditional powder blusher is best used on skin that has already had a powder finish i.e. you have applied your foundation and the set it with a powder, this ensures the blusher goes on smoothly without dragging the skin. Cream blushers are best applied to skin that has a tinted moisturiser or a light foundation only as the cream will be more blendable applying a cream blush to a powdered finished face will make the cheeks appear patchy. Gel blushers are great for a quick pick me up on bare moisturised skin but remember a little goes a long way. My favorite cream and powder blushers are both from *Ruby & Mille* with *Benefit* offering great gel blushers and highlighters

Bronzers are a great alternative to blushers, especially for women of colour, they add an instant glow that looks amazing in summer, there is no right or wrong way to apply bronzer however bronzing balls are easier to apply than gel bronzers as you can gradually build up the colour as you go. For a natural looking bronzer for darker skin tones have a look at the *Nars* range.

LIP COLOURS

As a black woman you will have more choices of what lip colours will look good on you than women of other races. Generally richer deeper colours look best on black women although some pale and frosty colours can sometimes work too.

If you have darker skin, deep red, fuchsia, magenta, chocolate brown and bronze will all compliment your skin tone. Medium skin tones suit reds, medium to deep pink, bronze, magenta and medium to deep brown. Fair shades suit pale to deep pink, peaches and nudes. Whichever skin tone you are do not be afraid to experiment with colours and cross over into different colour pallets.

Lip glosses are a more contemporary option to traditional lipsticks as they offer a more sheer coverage with some colour, for non sticky glosses chooses high quality brands such as *Bobbi Brown, MAC* and *Ruby & Mille*. To get the most out of your lipsticks, apply them with a brush for richer colour and a longer lasting finish.

Many make-up artists no longer recommend or use lip liners as they give too much of a polished look, for a more relaxed feel try applying lipstick or lip gloss then softening it with your fingers.

For those that like some variety there are many brands offering beautiful little lip pallets, these come with a combination of lipsticks and glosses in a colour palate that works together, don't be afraid to mix colours together to see what you like, some great lip pallets are *Bobbi Brown Basis Lips Pallet* and *Christian Dior Lip Palette.*

EYES

A perfectly groomed eyebrow will set of even the simplest look. Take a pencil and hold it against the edge of your nose, the start of your eyebrow should be in line with the tip of the pencil, now rotate the pencil at a 45º angle going along the centre of your iris, where the tip of the pencil meets your eyebrow is where the peak of your arch should be, now rotate the pencil further so it is in line with the corner of your eye, again where it meets your eyebrow this is where your eyebrow should end. With these three points in mind your eyebrows will always be perfectly balanced for your face. Make sure to check your eyebrows on a weekly basis to ensure any stray hairs are plucked away.

Changing the way you apply your eye make-up can dramatically change the appearance of your face. Simply by adjusting the colours you would normally use can bring a fresh youthful look to your appearance.

Whilst the most popular forms of eyeshadow are power based eyeshadows there are plenty of alternatives such a cream eyeshadows and loose pigments. Powder eyeshadows are most suited to general wear and are suitable for most skin types, you can build up the colour and layer colours to create different effects, powder eyeshadows to tend to crease along the socket line over the course of the day, a great product to prevent your eyeshadow from disappearing is *Urban Decay Potion Primer* this thick cream provides a base for your eyeshadow to cling on to allowing your eye make-up to last all day.

Loose pigments are great for a night time look, these rich intense colours are perfect for dark skin tones, by applying pigment with a damp brush will intensify the colour further, you can even try mixing the pigment with water and using a thin brush create an eyeliner in a similar colour to your eyeshadow.

Cream eye shadows are a very quick and convenient way of applying eye make-up, they are perfect for on the go make-up and are more suitable for more mature skins as they provide extra moisture.

Highlighters are a good way to add definition and make your perfectly groomed eyebrows stand out. Eyeliners also are another good way to add definition; they can be used alone or with a full eye look. Liquid eyeliners are the most dramatic and look great on dark skin, this forms a simple yet sophisticated look for day wear *Rimmel Exaggerate* and *MAC Fluidline* are great jet black liquid eyeliners for darker women.

Finally to finish off the look apply 2 coatings of a rich black mascara, the ultimate mascara has to be *Yves Saint Laurent Mascara Volume False Lash Effect Mascara* but this comes with a hefty price tag a more modest high end mascara is *Lancome Hypnose Mascara* or *Maybeline Great Lash Mascara* which is always a popular product, my personal favorite mascara has to be *L'Oreal Telescopic Clean Definition Mascara*. To get an even clump free finish wipe the wand on a clean tissue between each coat to prevent over build up.

BRUSHES

What you use to apply make-up is just as important as what make-up you apply. Using good quality make-up brushes will make the end result seem that more professional. In your make-up kit the most basic brushes you will need are:

A Foundation Brush	Used to apply foundation, primers and blend concealers into your base
A Powder Brush	For applying loose powder, pressed or oil absorbing powders or powder bronzers
A Blusher Brush	Used to apply blushers and highlighters to your cheeks
A Lip brush	For applying long lasting lipstick, this can also double up as a concealer brush
A Eye shadow Sponge	Used for applying the majority of your eye shadow
A Eye shadow Brush	For blending different eye shadows together
A Eyebrow Brush	To shape and groom your eyebrows
A Eyelash Comb	Used to separate your eyelashes after applying mascara

Many professional makeup artist insist on using *MAC* and *Nars* brushes these can range from £7 - £32 each, however there are some good quality brushes available on the high street such *the Body Shop* make-up brush range and brushes from *The Make-up Brush Company*. Store them in a fold away pouch for travel or an upright container for ease of access.

It is important to keep your brushes clean to prevent bacteria from building up as this can lead to spots and blemishes on your skin, there are specialist brush cleaners on the market however washing them once or twice a week with an antibacterial hand wash or facial wash is just as effective at removing stubborn make-up, wash them in warm water and leave them to dry naturally. To keep your make-up free of bacteria; lightly spray your eyeshadows, lipsticks, blushers etc with a highly concentrated surgical spirit, as this evaporates every quickly it will not ruin your make-up; even powder based make up.

APPLICATION

Make-up should always be applied to clean skin, if possible wait 30 minutes after cleansing and moisturising your skin before you begin to apply any make-up, this will allow your skin to settle down and for your moisturiser to be absorbed into your skin, oily areas can be left bare to prevent your make-up from becoming too oily. Ensure your fingers are clean and you have all of your tools to hand. For ultimate staying power prime your face and eyelids first and apply a light coating of your favorite lip balm to your lips.

Start off with your foundation or tinted moisturiser followed by concealer if you need it; be sure to blend thoroughly especially at the jaw line, hair line and around your nose. Do not go too heavy with your base otherwise your make-up will look too thick and mask like; you should still be able to see your natural skin through the make-up. Then take a tissue and blot off any excess oil or foundation from your skin.

Next move onto the eyes, if you are applying heavy eye make-up dust a thick layer of loose powder to the upper areas of your checks this will catch any excess eyeshadow and prevent it from ruining your base that you have just applied. Apply a brow gel or clear mascara to your eyebrows to hold them in place after filling them in with a dark brown eye shadow or eyebrow pencil if it is needed.

Many women have trouble with applying eyeliner particularly liquid eyeliner to the top eyelids. If this is you then try drawing small lines starting off with the middle of your eyelid working out towards the outer edge with your eye semi closed, then go back and join up the lines. The trick is to use short firm lines in one fluid movement so you get a nice straight line rather than a jagged one. Another trick to create the 'cat eye' look is to draw elongated triangles out from the corners of your eyes then blend it into the main line of your eyeliner, this may take a few goes before you get it right so be patient. To draw attention to your eyes try using a light reflecting eyeshadow to the inner corners of your eyes and blend above and below your lashes.

To finish off your eyes apply 2 coats of mascara. Mascara is easier to apply if you apply it whilst looking down into a small hand mirror, start of at the base getting a firm grip between the brush and your lashes and wiggle as you reach the tip wait a few seconds before looking up otherwise you will smudge and ruin your eye shadow. Next apply your lip colour, remember if you have gone heavy on the eyes go light or nude on the lips and of you have a heavy lip colour go for a simple eye, never go heavy with both. Finally finish off with your favorite blusher or bronzer, judging the intensity to suit the rest of your make-up.

REMOVING MAKE-UP

Cleansing your skin thoroughly before you go to sleep is very important, as your skin repairs itself each night it is important that it is not hindered in any way, wearing make-up to bed will block your skins renewal process leading to blackheads and spots.

Most products on the market will not cleanse your skin thoroughly enough; you will find some traces of dirt or make-up still left on your skin after washing. This is why it is beneficial to remove make-up first with an oil based make-up remover. This will melt away make-up particularly mascara leaving you with a semi clean face to continue with your cleansing. Cleansing your face with an oil based cleanser can be very beneficial to your skin as some cleansers may be strip away your natural oils; applying an oil to your skin will create an additional barrier (like pre-shampooing). Alternatively you can use a natural plant oil such as jojoba or castor oil; which is known the help thicken up eyelashes and eyebrow so this is often an oil that is frequently used on the eye area.

Thoroughly massage in your chosen oil all over your face and eye area the take a piece of cotton wool and wipe away the oil, repeat if you are wearing a heavy foundation or eye make-up or until the cotton wool comes away virtually clean. Now you can follow up with your regular cleanser confident that all of your make-up and oil will be removed before you go to sleep.

BODY CARE

SKIN CONDITIONS

KELOIDS

Keloids are scars that have gone several steps too far; they become raised from the surface of the skin and are irregular in shape. Unlike other scars Keloids do not fade over time and have to be professionally removed from the skin.

Keloids may take some time to appear after an injury occurs and can spread slightly to unaffected areas near to the wound. They tend to appear after surgery or injury; they can also be triggered after piercing burns and minor abrasions.

Keloids are more common amongst people of colour and are found to be common amongst people of the same family. They are more likely to form on the chest, back, shoulders and earlobes but very rarely appear on the face.

If you are aware that you or your other family members are prone to Keloid scarring then take care to prevent getting them in the first place as although there are some treatments to remove them many of these treatments are unsuccessful and often lead to the Keloid becoming much bigger.

Cortisone injections are able to flatten Keloids somewhat by injecting a small dose of steroids directly into the scar, these injections can make the scar more red in colour but this redness can be treated with several pulsed-dye laser treatments. The Keloid will look a lot smaller than it was to start with but it will still be fairly visible.

HYPERPIGMENTATION

Hyperpigmentation is a common skin condition in which some patches of skin turn darker in colour. This is a harmless condition caused when there is too much brown pigment, Melanin, in the skin. This condition can affect people in all races but is more common in people of colour.

The most common reason for Hyperpigmentation amongst people of colour is from spots, blemishes or Acne. When the skin is irritated or inflamed Hyperpigmentation can occur as part of the healing process. Exposure to the sun can cause Hyperpigmentation to become more visible this is why sunscreen is so important to people of colour.

Many black women are tempted to seek out skin lightening creams to correct Hyperpigmentation; a lot of these creams contain many harmful ingredients such as Hydroquinone which has been linked to several cases of Leukaemia. Hydroquinone breaks down the skins Melanin production which leaves the skin vulnerable to the suns UV rays. Therefore creams containing Hydroquinone should not be used and are in fact banned within Europe.

An effective method for lessening Hyperpigmentation is to keep blemishes to a minimum and to wear plenty of sunscreen daily. Exfoliation and Microdermabrasion (which is a more intensive form of Exfoliation) is proven to lessen the visibility of Hyperpigmentation if done on a regular basis. *Bio-Oil* is a fantastic scar fading oil that can be purchased from high street chemists, by applying the oil daily to a scar or area that is highly pigmented will dramatically improve the condition and overall look of the area. Diluted apple cider vinegar is another effective method of fading the Hyperpigmentation and evening out the skin tone as is lemon juice, apply this as you would a toner daily until you see an improvement.

ACNE

Acne is caused by over activity of the Sebaceous glands that secrete Sebum (your skins natural oil) on to your skin. The Sebaceous glands of people with Acne are especially sensitive to normal blood levels of a hormone called Testosterone, found naturally in both men and women.

The Testosterone triggers the Sebaceous glands to produce too much Sebum. During this time, the dead skin cells lining the opening of the hair follicles are not shed properly therefore and clog the follicles. The combination the excess oil and trapped skin cells cause a build up in your pores which cause blackheads and whiteheads to form. For most people the problem stops here but for others this build ups leads to the growth of a bacteria called Propionibacterium Acnes which is what creates the red inflamed areas. This can then lead to Cysts which in turn rupture and causes scaring and Hyperpigmentation.

Acne is not due to diet or hygiene it is an imbalance of hormonal activity and this can be hereditary. As acne cannot be cured the only possible course of action is to control the symptoms before they erupt. Keep the skin clean by washing twice a day using a mild cleanser such as *Cetaphil*, next you will need to kill the harmful bacterial which is causing the Acne, creams that are high in Benzoyl Peroxide (4-5%) such as *Oxy on the Spot Treatment* or one prescribed by your doctor are perfect for this, use a generous amount and thoroughly cover the affected area. Benzoyl Peroxide will dry out your skin immensely but this is part of the healing process, it is important to follow up with a rich moisturising cream with an SPF. Another option is to use a mild liquid exfoliator on a regular bases to loosen the dead skin from the follicles.

ECZEMA & DRY SKIN

Eczema is a skin condition that causes the skin to become inflamed and very itchy, it is also known as Atopic Eczema as well as Atopic Dermatitis. It usually starts in childhood during the first six months of life, over the years the Eczema can flare up and calm down and stresses in life can bring on flare ups more regularly. Eczema is most common on the joints and folds on the body such as the backs of the knees, inner arms and neck.

Some Eczema suffers may also experience Hay Fever and Asthma, these are grouped together in a complex known as Atopy. Eczema is different from one person to another as it affects 10 -15% of the population there is no quick fix cure. Eczema suffers often find relief by using creams containing Hydrocortisone; which is an anti-inflammatory steroid cream, it sooths the itchy feeling and calms down the inflamed skin.

Taking oatmeal infused hot baths will also help to hydrate the skin, add a scoop of oatmeal into a muslin bag and hang from the tap, the water will run through the bag adding the benefits if the oatmeal to the water, you can even try using the wet bag as a sponge directly on the area.

It is important to keep your hands well moisturised as this is one area that is constantly exposed to the elements which could make the Eczema worse, keep an unscented moisturiser in your bag and moisturise whenever you feel the need, unrefined organic Shea Butter is a very rich cream that contains no irritating ingredients.

When treating Eczema, it is a good idea to keep in mind this saying that Dermatologist often refer to "If it's wet, dry it. If it's dry, wet it" meaning areas that are weeping or oozing a clear substance; dry them out with gel form medications rather than creams and dry cracked areas are best treated with thicker moisturising creams and ointments. When treating Eczema on the whole rich creams are more affective on the majority of area rather than gels.

Eczema can be dealt with to a reasonable level if you keep up with the moisturising and do not scratch the affected area as scratching leads to open wounds and infections, try sleeping with clean cotton gloves to help prevent itching.

TOP TO TOE

Your skin is the largest organ of your body; it sheds and renews itself every 21 days. By looking after your skin you can ensure that it looks as youthful as possible for as long as possible.

Regular exfoliation can ensure your skin is kept smooth and radiant and also boosts the blood circulation. The simplest and most effective way to exfoliate your skin is to use exfoliating gloves in the bath or shower with your regular soap or shower gel. There are some great ready made exfoliating products for the body such as *the Sanctuary Salt Scrub* or *the Sanctuary Nourishing Hot Sugar Scrub* which is an amazing scrub that warms up on contact with your skin.

Moisturising your skin is just as important as moisturising you face, be sure to use a moisturiser with added SPF when exposed to sunlight. Look for rich moisturising creams particularly for problem areas such as the feet, knees and elbows. Some great creams are *the Body Shop Vitamin E Body Butter* and *Johnson & Johnson 24 Hour Moisture Body Cream with Shea Butter*. Be sure to moisturise your hands and neck as much as possible as these are areas that dry out the quickest and show age the fastest.

Your feet are another area that needs special care and attention regular pedicures can dramatically improve the condition and comfort of your hardworking feet. Prepare your feet first by removing any hardened skin with a foot file such as *the Ped Egg* which is a great tool for safely removing hard skin. Then soak your feet in warm to hot water and exfoliate with an exfoliating scrub such as *the Body Shop Peppermint Soothing Foot Scrub* followed with a luxurious moisturising cream such as *the Body Shop Hemp Foot Protector*. Finally trim and file your toe nails and follow up with 2 coats a vibrant nail polish.

EXERCISE

Keeping your body active is an important part of staying healthy and supple, regular exercise can ensure that your body is at the optimal weight for its height and helps keep everything working how it is supposed to.

Exercise does not have to be very intense or time consuming; it can be something as simple as a brisk 30 minute walk, dancing on a night out or vigorous house work. Aim to do a minimum of three 30 minutes active sessions per week. Vary your routine so your body does not get overly used to one type of exercise.

As you get older exercise is even more important as it helps your muscles and joints work at their best preventing unnecessary injury. Yoga, Pilates and Swimming are great exercise choices for many woman and is suitable for many ages.

FRAGRANCE

Choosing a fragrance that suits you can be a difficult task. You may have smelt a perfume on a friend that you and admired but the fragrance did not quite smell the same on you, this is because each person's skin is different and has its own natural pH balance and natural scent.

To choose a signature scent firstly decide which of the six categories you are more drawn towards, Oriental; musky incenses fragrances, Chypre; fresh nature fragrances, Fougere; fragrances of herbs and spices, Florals; bouquet of fresh flowers Citrus; zesty scents or Ozonic; fragrances of the ocean. Now you can look in more detail what ingredients in those types of scents you like such as hints of sandalwood and cedar in woody musky fragrances or rose fragrances in floral tones.

Once you have narrowed down what you like, you will have to take note of how the fragrance changes. Perfumes have 3 types of scent which is referred to as a note. Top notes are what you smell immediately after applying the perfume; it is quite strong and fades very quickly. Middle notes last a bit longer; and linger for approximately an hour. Finally the base note blends with the middle note to form the main bulk of the perfume; this is a richer scent and lasts for several hours or until you reapply. Perfumes should be stored out of direct sunlight and preferably in a dark box away from heat to protect the fragrance.

Some stores offer a create your own fragrance range where you can purchase 2 or 3 fragrances and layer them on top of each other to create your own perfume. There are many luxury perfumeries that specialise in this and can create a one off perfume just for you. One of the most exclusive perfumeries is *Harrods Haute Parfumerie Fifth Floor Urban Retreat* where you can sit in luxury as someone creates the perfect fragrance for just for you.

PRODUCT LIST

Shampoos

ApHogee Deep Moisture Shampoo
ApHogee Shampoo for Damaged Hair
Aveda Detox Shampoo
Aveda Sap Moss Shampoo
Cream of Nature Moisturising Shampoo
Elasta QP Cream Conditioning Shampoo
Giovanni Smooth as Silk Shampoo
Kenra Clarifying Shampoo
KeraCare Dry & Itchy Scalp Shampoo
Neutrogena Triple Moisture Cream Lather
Nexxus Aloe Rid Shampoo
Organix Nourishing Coconut Milk Shampoo
Pantene Pro-V Purity Shampoo
Shampoo Three' by Paul Mitchell
Shikakai Shampoo bars

Deep Moisturising Conditioners

Alter Ego Garlic Treatment Oil Conditioner
Aveda Sap Moss Conditioning detangle
Aubrey Organics Honeysuckle Rose Conditioner
Aubrey Organics White Camellia Conditioner
Biolage Ultra Hydrating Conditioning Balm
Crème Of Nature Nourishing Conditioner
Elucence Moisture Balancing Conditioner
Jason Natural Thin -Thick hair & Scalp Therapy
Extra Volume Conditioner
Jason Natural Jojoba Conditioner
Jason Natural Biotin Conditioner

KeraCare Humecto
Kenra Moisturizing Conditioner
Lustrasilk Shea Butter Cholesterol Plus Mango
Mizani Moisturefuse
Mizani Thermasmooth
Neutrogena Triple Moisture Mask
Redken All Soft Heavy Cream
Salerm 21 Wheat Germ Mask
Queen Helene Cholesterol
Ultra Black Hair Deep Conditioner

Protein Conditioners

Affirm 5 in 1 Reconstructor
ApHogee Keratin 2 Minute Reconstructor
ApHogee Treatment for Damaged Hair
Aubrey Organics GPB Balancing Conditioner
Biolage Fortetherapie Cera-Repair Treatment
Creme Of Nature Conditioning Reconstructor
Elucence Extended Moisture Repair Treatment
Jason Natural Lavender Strengthening Conditioner
Joico K Pak Deep Penetrating Reconstructor
Kenra Platinum Shea Butter Reconstructor
Mizani Fulfyl Conditioning Treatment
Nature's Gate Biotin Strengthening Conditioner
Nexxus Emergencee
Organics Hair Mayonnaise Treatment for Damaged Hair
Organic Root Stimulator Hair Mayonnaise
Ultra Sheen Duo Tex Protein Conditioner

Leave-In Conditioners
Aubrey Organic Honeysuckle Rose Conditioner
Aubrey Organics White Camellia Conditioner
Aussie Miracle Hair Insurance Leave In.
Crème of Nature Leave in cream
Dove Daily Moisture Mist
Elasta QP Mango Butter
Infusium 23
Neutrogena Triple Moisture Silky Touch Leave In
Pantene Smoothing Cream
Sebastian Originals Potion 9
VO5 Miracle Mist Leave In

Oils
Africa's Best Herbal Oil
Almond oil
Alma oil
Avocado oil
Carrot oil
Castor oil
Coconut oil
Jojoba oil
KeraCare Essential oils
Olive oil
Shea Butter
Sweet Almond oil
Vatika oil

Electrical Hair Tools
Bespoke Labs Tourmaline T3 Evolution Hair Dryer
Brazilian Heat Tourmaline Ceramic Curling Iron
CHI Rocket Professional Hair Dryer
Farouk Biosilk Straightening Iron
FHI Platform Straighteining Iron
GHD Straighteining Iron
Gold N Hot Professional Ceramic Marcel Iron
Maxiglide Straighteining Iron
Pibbs Kwik Dri Hooded Dryer 514
Rusk's Ceramic Str8 Straighteining Iron
Sedu Pro Nano Straighteining Iron
Vidal Sasson Hot Tools Hair Straightener

Skincare
African Black Soap
Aveeno Clear Complexion Cream Cleanser
Aveeno Positively Radiant Cleanser
Aveeno Positively Radiant SPF 30 Moisturiser
Clarisonic Skin Cleansing System
Clarins Multi Active Day Cream
Clinique Dramatically Difference Moisturiser
Clinique 3 Step Skin Care System
Himani Turmeric Cream
Liz Earle Hot Polish cleanser
Lush Coalface Cleanser Bar Soap
Neutrogena Liquid Facial Cleansing Formula
Neutrogena Visibly Even Foaming Cleanser
Origins Checks and Balance Facial Wash
Origins Get Down Facial Wash
Origins Never A Dull Moment Facial Wash
Pro-Activ Face Wash

Make-Up
Bobbi Brown
ColourLab
MAC
Make Up Forever
Prescriptives
Ruby & Mille
Smashbox

Body Skincare
Aveno
L'Occitane
Lush Dream Cream
Natural oils
Neutrogena
Shea Butter
The Sanctuary

SUMMARY

As women of colour our beauty practices will differ from women of other races, this makes it difficult to find useful and relevant information that we can incorporate into our everyday lives. Many women of colour experience difficulties with their hair and skin care and often find nowhere to turn to find valuable answers to problems that are quite easily resolved.

The Afro Hair & Beauty Bible aims to resolve common beauty problems that black women face in an easy to read and practical form. If you have any comments about the book you can post a message at www.theafrohairandbeautybible.co.uk where you can also keep updated about future titles and their release dates.

Looking good on the outside helps you feel good on the inside, if you feel good you can tackle any obstacle the world throws has to throw at you!

USEFUL RESOURCES

www.afrotherapy.com
Ethnic beauty tips and advice for Afro hair, Skin care and make-up

www.akamuti.co.uk
100% hair and skincare natural products

www.anitagrant.com
Organic skin and hair care

www.bellaonline.com
Advice and tips on cosmetics and information on the cosmetic industry for women of colour

www.clarisonic.com
The Skincare System

www.denmanbrush.com
Buy Denman brushes online

www.drugstore.com
Buy hair and skin products online, international shipping

www.ebonexxus.com
A website dedicated to women of colour

www.ernolaszlo.com
Erno Laszlo Skincare System

www.hqhair.com
Buy hair and skin products online, international shipping

www.indianhaircompany.com
Top quality Indian human hair

www.kevynaucoindirect.com
High quality make-up from the celebrity make-up artist for all races

www.makeupalley.com
Online beauty community

www.rxforbrownskin.com
Skin care line for dark skin formulated by dermatologist Dr Susan Taylor

www.samfine.com
Celebrity Make Up Artist

www.treasuredlocks.com
Products and information on Afro haircare

NOTES

THE
AFRO
HAIR
BEAUTY &
BIBLE

NOTES

THE
AFRO
HAIR
BEAUTY &
BIBLE